AF484480

Pandemic Press Media Magazine

Summer 2023 Volume 2, Issue 1

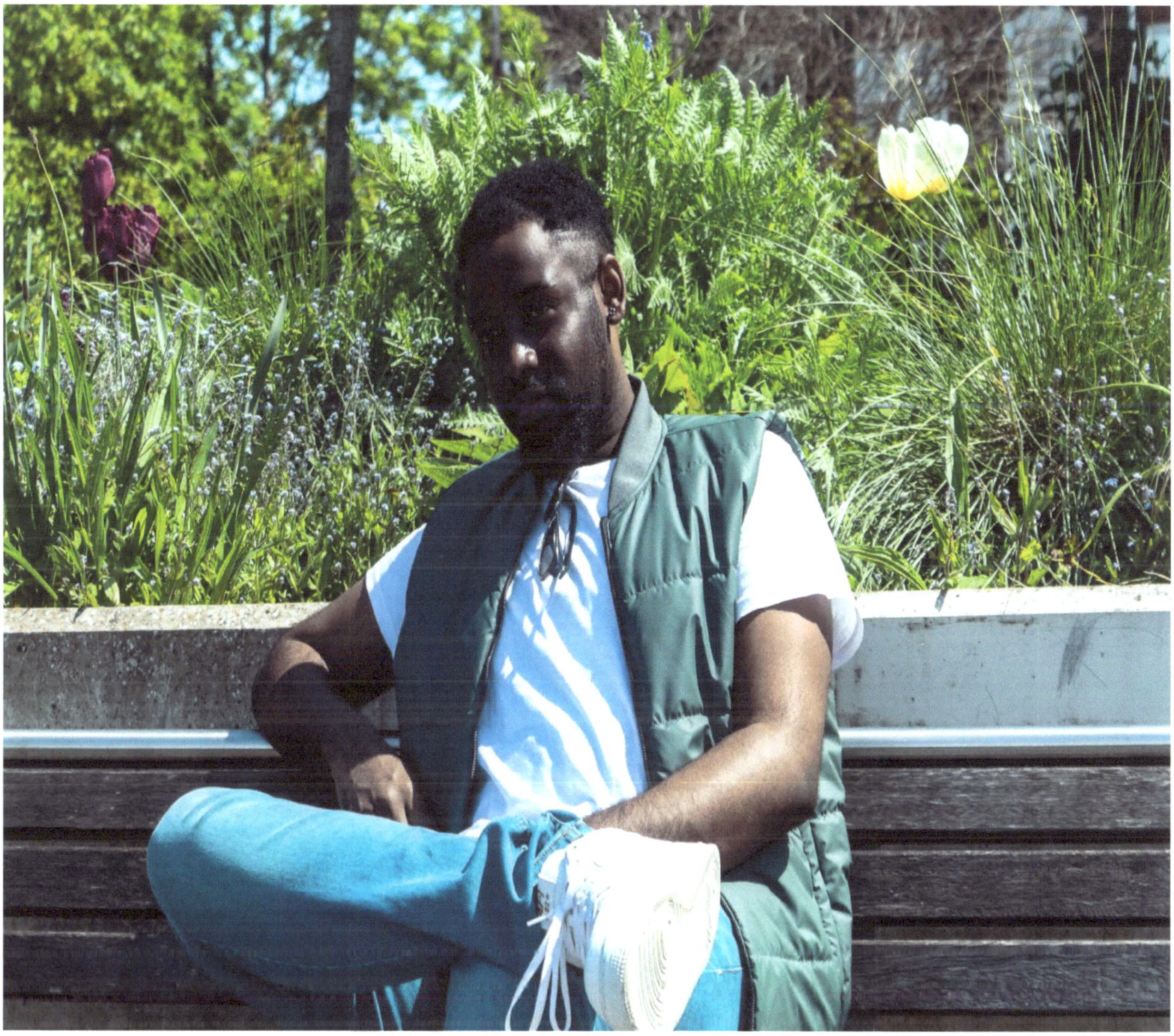

Inside This Issue:

1. Letter From The Editors
2. Cover Story- One on One with FEGS!!
3. Cooking Fun w/ Mrs. Cubbage
4. The Music Spotlight w/ Sam C. Smooth
5. At the Movies
6. Advice Column
7. Advertise With Us
8. Sam C On Sports
9. Fitness Facts
10. The CUBB House Merch Store
11. Let's Read
12. Pandemic Press Publishing
13. Radio Show Spotlight
14. Writing Help
15. Thank You
16. Share Ideas
17. Connect With Us On Social Media
18. Our Sponsor: Vybrant Souls (Health and Wellness)

Letter From The Editors

Welcome back to Pandemic Press Media Magazine- a cultural and lifestyle magazine!! Brought to you by Pandemic Press Media, LLC! Thank you for joining us for the Summer 2023 Edition! (This magazine is a quarterly publication.) This is the first of our SECOND VOLUME! We are VERY excited!!

We are dedicated to bringing you the best information, cover stories, feature stories, reviews, music, sports and more! We will also begin tapping into the lives of positive, industry leaders!

Also, if there is something that we aren't reporting that you would like to see, please let us know!

Sincerely,

Samuel and Bobbie Cubbage

Cover Story

One on One with FEGS!

We were blessed to have Gospel Music Artist FEGS stop by PPM Magazine for a one on one interview!

PPM Magazine: Hi, FEGS! Thank you for joining us! Could you tell our readers about yourself?

FEGS: My name is FEGS, which stands for 'F'or'E'ver 'G'od's 'S'on, and I am a gospel artist and producer from South London in the UK.

PPM Magazine: Tell us about your music.

FEGS: I make Gospel music that is genuinely Birthed Out Of The Spirit Of God. My music crosses between different genres; but the message is the same, the Gospel Of Jesus Christ.

PPM Magazine: How did you get started in this field?

FEGS: I started playing the drums in my dad's church as a kid, and then later began to play other instruments such as the piano and guitar. Around 10 years ago, I heard my pastor at the time say, if God is blessing you with songs, then write them down, and since then I've been writing.

PPM Magazine: What is your motivation?

FEGS: I wouldn't say it's a matter of what, but a matter of who, and that person is God.

PPM Magazine: If you could work with anyone in the world, who would it be and why?

FEGS: Thankfully I have a great team of gifted people around me, so I feel like I'm working with the people I'd like to work with.

PPM Magazine: Who is your mentor?
FEGS: God.

PPM Magazine: Yes! Absolutely! Tell us a little bit about your latest track, "Ocean Divider"?

FEGS: My new single **Ocean Divider** is a praise and worship song, and a testimony as to how much God looks out for everyone and takes them 'through the fire'.

The term 'Ocean Divider' reminds us of how God parted the sea to deliver the Children of Israel from Pharaoh; reminding us all to have faith in the midst of all the chaos and darkness, knowing that God is always there for us.

Ocean Divider is influenced by the Scripture Psalm 68:4 'Sing unto God, Sing praises to His name: extol Him that rideth upon the heavens by His name JAH, and rejoice before Him.'

I wrote this song when I was wondering if things were going to change and I knew that ultimately God would see me through it. The Guide through the storm, He's the 'Ocean Divider'.

PPM Magazine: Amen! And it's so inspirational! If someone wanted to reach out to you, how would they do it?
**FEGS**: Follow me on social media @FEGSDOE, and send me a message.

PPM Magazine: Any shoutouts?

**FEGS**: Shout out to the team at Music Birthed Out Of The Spirit.

PPM Magazine: Thank you so much FEGS for sitting down and talking with us! It was our pleasure!

Cooking Fun with Mrs. Cubbage!!

Helloooooo, Everybody!! I'm so happy to have you here! I'm Mrs. Cubbage! I am an author, early childhood educator, wife, daughter, sister, friend, podcaster, certified life coach and entrepreneur! One thing I love doing is teaching! Teaching people. Especially young people. One thing that I really enjoy is teaching young people how to cook. Once they master that skill; along with gaining the confidence to excel in the kitchen, everything else that they try to do is easy! New episodes of my show are available Fridays at 4PM EST on The CCI Radio Show YouTube Channel!

Here are a few recipes from my book, "Plan-demic Meals: Meal planning during the Covid-19 Pandemic" that you and your family are sure to LOVE!

Garlic Shrimp and Kale

Ingredients:

2 Cloves of Fresh Garlic (Minced)
3 Bags of Extra Large Shrimp
2 Bunches of Kale (Chopped)
2 large Tomatoes (Chopped)
Olive oil
½ Yellow Onion (Minced)
½ tbs Seasoning Salt
Pepper (to taste)
1 Red Pepper (Chopped)
Fresh Basil (to taste)
Fresh Parsley (to taste)
½ tbs Italian Seasoning
3 Pats of Butter

Directions:

In a medium skillet, add 1 pat of butter. When the butter is melted, add the kale. Saute the kale for about 5 minutes. Add the chopped tomatoes to the skillet. Add a lid and allow the kale and tomatoes to cook for about five minutes. In a large skillet, add 2 pats of butter. When the butter is melted, saute the garlic, red pepper and onion. Add the contents from that medium skillet to the larger skillet. Add 2 teaspoons of water, add the lip and let simmer while deveining the shrimp.
When the shrimp is clean, add the olive oil to the medium skillet, and saute the shrimp for 4 minutes total. Add the shrimp to the larger skillet, add the basil, Italian seasoning, and pepper. Mix lightly. Serve warm. Enjoy!

The fun thing about cooking with children is exposing them to more veggies. This next recipe is the PERFECT mix of fun and flavor that the kids will LOVE!

Veggie Pasta with Red Peppers and Kale

Ingredients:

½ Red Pepper (chopped)
1 cup of Kale (chopped)
½ cup Red Onions (chopped)
1 clove Fresh Garlic (minced)
Veggie Pasta
2 'pats' of Butter
1 pint container of Grape Tomatoes (cut each in half- horizontally)
1 sprig of Fresh Basil (chopped)

Dash of fresh Black Pepper
Salt to taste

Directions:

In a large pot, boil 3 cups of water. Once the water is bright to a boil (about 7 minutes), add veggie pasta. In a large skillet, add 2 pats of butter. When the butter has melted, add red onions, garlic and red peppers. Saute for 3 minutes, until soft. Turn the heat down to low. Add kale and tomatoes. Let simmer for about 5 minutes. Mix while simmering. Add fresh basil. At this point, the pasta should be finished. Drain the water off of the pasta. Add the pasta to the skillet. Mix for about 2 minutes- until the vegetables and pasta are mixed well. Add a dash of salt and pepper to taste. Enjoy!

Pandemic
Press
Publishing

Cubbage Connection Inc
RADIO SHOW
Globally Connected

PANDEMIC
PRESS
MEDIA

The Music Spotlight w/ Sam C. Smooth

Welcome to The Music Spotlight! I'm Sam C Smooth! This is where you'll find all of the latest music news and my picks for the best music for this issue of our magazine.

Music News: Gospel Music Artist FEGS recently released his newest single, "Ocean Divider!" This is a great, inspirational and motivational song! Make sure you find it now on all music platforms!

Let's get started with the music picks for this edition of our magazine!

Love Notes Top 10 Albums

1. II-Boyz II Men
2. The Velvet Rope-Janet Jackson
3. Lady Soul-Aretha Franklin
4. Songs In The Key Of Life-Stevie Wonder
5. Love Deluxe-Sade
6. After Hours-The Weekend
7. Whitney-Whitney Houston
8. Sign O' The Times-Prince
9. What's Going On-Marvin Gaye
10. Crazy Sexy Cool-TLC

Love Notes Top 10 Singles

1. Let's Stay Together-Al Green
2. Love On Top-Beyonce
3. All of Me-John Legend
4. Ain't Nobody-Chaka Khan
5. Be My Baby-The Ronettes
6. Nothing Else Matters-Lauryn Hill
7. When A Man Loves A Woman-Percy Sledge
8. I Want To Love What Love Is-Foreigner
9. Where Is The Love-Roberta Flack and Donny Hathaway
10. My Girl-The Temptations

Gospel Excellence Top 10 Albums

1. Love Unstoppable- Fred Hammond
2. Impossible- Pastor Mike Jr.
3. All Things New- Tye Tribbett
4. God Period- E. Dewey Smith
5. Believe For It- Cece Winans
6. When You Speak- Jeremy Camp
7. Light Will Find You- Antoine Bradford
8. Endless Praise- Charity Gayle
9. Ghetto Gospel-Red Wave
10. Long, Live, Love- Kirk Franklin

Gospel Excellence Top 10 Singles

1. Ocean Divider-FEGS
2. Shackles-Mary Mary
3. We Fall Down-Donnie McClurkin
4. Pray-Mc Hammer
5. Marvin Sapp-Never Would Have Made It
6. Won't Be Moved- Gene Moore
7. Making Room Live- Ricky Dillard
8. The Table- Jonathan Taylor
9. Every Praise- Hezekiah Walker
10. Jesus Is Love- The Commodores

Back To The 80s Podcast Top 10 Albums

1. Purple Rain- Prince And The Revolution
2. Bad-Michael Jackson
3. True Blue-Madonna
4. Remain In Light- Talking Heads
5. Faith-George Michael
6. Private Dancer-Tina Dancer
7. Appetite For Destruction-Guns N Roses
8. So- Peter Gabriel
9. Get Happy- Elvis Costello
10. Born In The USA- Bruce Springsteen

Back To The 80s Top 10 Singles

1. Walk This Way- Aerosmith/Run DMC
2. Livin' On A Prayer- Bon Jovi
3. Tainted Love- Soft Cell
4. The Rain- Oran "Juice" Jones
5. Rumors- Timex Social Club
6. Say Say Say- Paul McCartney/Michael Jackson
7. Mr. Telephone Man- New Edition
8. Mickey- Toni Basil
9. Foolish Heart- Steve Perry
10. Fame- Irene Cara

Back To The 90s Podcast Top 10 Albums

1. The Miseducation Of Lauryn Hill- Lauryn Hill
2. The Chronic- Dr Dre
3. Baduizm-Erykah Badu
4. Life After Death- The Notorious BIG
5. Automatic For The People- REM
6. Jagged Little Pill- Alanis Morrisette
7. Supa Dupa Fly- Missy Elliott
8. Illmatic- NAS
9. The Downward Spiral- Nine Inch Nails
10. Doggystyle- Snoop Dogg

Back To The 90s Podcast Top 10 Singles

1. I'm Too Sexy- Right Said Fred
2. No Diggity- Blackstreet
3. I Want It That Way- Backstreet Boys
4. Wannabe- Spice Girls
5. I Swear- All 4 One
6. Black Velvet- Alannah Myles
7. Semi Charmed Life- Third Eye Blind
8. Vision Of Love- Mariah Carey
9. The Boy Is Mine- Brandy/Monica
10. Hold On-En Vogue

That's it for now! Make sure to listen to The CCI Radio Show Audio Podcasts: Love Notes, Gospel Excellence, The Back To The 80s Podcast and the soon to be debuting The Back To The 90s Podcast! They're all available on Blogtalkradio and where podcasts are available! See you in the next edition with more music picks and news!

At the Movies with Bobbie D.

Welcome to "At the Movies with Bobbie D"! If you've been purchasing our magazine and have read my reviews of movies, one thing you have noticed is that I'm a true movie buff! I LOVE going to and watching movies!

And I am going to give you my opinion of a "cult classic"...

"Revenge of the Nerds (the original)"! (1984)

Revenge of the nerds is a great movie! It's a movie about the 'underdogs' getting their 'revenge' so to speak...lol! It's an uplifting tale that truly weaves the comedy and tragedy of college life through the eyes of a "nerd"!

This movie is a comedy that shows how nerds were treated at a fictional school in the 1980's. However, the nerds are HIGHLY intelligent, and come up with some creative ways to get revenge on their bullies. I will not spoil this movie for you; however, if you haven't seen it, make sure that you do!

TLC Advice Column

Thank you for joining us. This is a place where you can express your feelings and issues, without judgment.

Hello! Thank you so much for reading my letter.

My best friend doesn't take me seriously. And I believe that she isn't going to be in my life for very much longer.

My reasons for thinking this is my career path is on the rise! She's watching this happen for me, but supporting others who are doing similar things. I've tried to bring her into my new circle (to help career), she poo-poos EVERYTHING I do. It's very frustrating. I have fun with her; we have been friends for years. But, how can she support others and not me? She even travels to other places to show her support for others. What should I do?

Thank you so much for reaching out to us! We understand what you are going through. The saying is true, "People are in your life for a reason, a season or a lifetime." This friend sounds like she is in your life for a 'season'. We're sure that she is fun and you have love for each other. It sounds like things have been going well...until you began to elevate. This is very upsetting. I would talk to her to find out where her mind might be (just so you are sure). If you do not like what you hear, it may be time to begin slowly pulling away. If the people closest to you don't appreciate what you are doing, they aren't the right people in your life. We hope that this helps. Please keep us posted on what's going on.

If you need advice, and don't know where to turn, reach out to us at pandemicpm@gmail.com. Please include in the subject line" TLC Advice."

Thank you for your support. We invite you to follow and connect with our YouTube Channel, The CCI Radio Show. Please like, click, share and subscribe. You can also listen to our secondary shows, The CCI Radio Show "Gospel Excellence w/ The Angel of the Airwaves, Bobbie D," The CCI Radio Show "Love Notes w/ Sam C Smooth", The CCI Radio Show "Back To The 80s Podcast" and "Back to the 90s Podcast" on Blogtalkradio, Soundcloud, Spotify, Anchor Podcasts and many other social media outlets. The CCI Radio Show "TLC Podcast" is also available on our YouTube Channel!

Pandemic Press Media
ADVERTISE WITH US
Email us
at
pandemicpm@
gmail.com
for rates
and details!

Sam C On Sports

*Hello and welcome to Sam C on Sports for this edition of our magazine! I will give you the sports news and info! ***Please note: some of the sports news may have already changed from the time of this magazine publication!*** Let's get started!*

MLB: The Major League Baseball season is getting closer to the halfway point of the season. One of the hottest teams right now are the Pittsburgh Pirates! They started the season off redhot. They have had some

stumbles recently. But, they have still managed to be one of the best teams in baseball, sitting atop the NL Central Division. Some other teams on a winning streak right now are The Tampa Bay Rays, The LA Dodgers, the Atlanta Braves and the Texas Rangers. This season is getting very good and competitive! This will be exciting to see what happens after the All Star Break in the weeks to come!

NFL: The NFL Draft has come and gone! This year's ceremony was held in Kansas City, the home of the current Super Bowl champs, the Kansas City Chiefs. It was another exciting draft with many of today's promising stars having their dreams fulfilled as teams selected them one by one. Of course, there were many players selected after the draft was over. Some notable names selected in the draft include Bryce Young, University of Alabama Quarterback selected by the Carolina Panthers and C.J. Stroud, Ohio State University Quarterback. Both were selected numbers 1 and 2 in the first round. Many teams also made a lot of acquisitions during the NFL free agency period. The preseason begins in August. Training camps start in July. We also want to send our thoughts and prayers to the family of NFL great, Jim Brown. He passed away peacefully on May 18th, 2023 at the age of 87. He was possibly the greatest running back of all time and the greatest Cleveland Brown of all time.

NHL: The hockey season is currently in the playoffs! There are 4 teams left, fighting to win the Stanley Cup. They are the Carolina Hurricanes, the Vegas Golden Knights, the Dallas Stars and the Florida Panthers! One of these teams will be celebrating with the trophy soon. Good luck to the last teams standing!

USFL: The USFL season is at the halfway point! We've seen a lot of great games so far. It's hard to believe that the playoffs will be coming soon. Hopefully, your team will make it and will win the championship. Good luck to all of the teams!

XFL: The XFL season just wrapped up a week ago. We have a champion. Congrats to the Arlington Renegades! They defeated the DC Defenders 35-26 to win the XFL title! What's impressive about this is that Arlington went into the playoffs with a losing record, 4-6. They defeated the top team, the Defenders, who had a record of 9-1. It was a great season!

NBA: The NBA is also in playoff mode. We have the LA Lakers, Denver Nuggets, Boston Celtics and Miami Heat as the last 4 teams standing. The Lakers and the Nuggets are surprise teams that entered the playoffs. These are great matchups so let's see which one of these teams wins it all!

WNBA: As stated last time, the biggest storyline in the WNBA is the safe return of Brittney Griner from captivity in Russia. She is back and played in her first game, preseason recently in a losing effort. She is back in rare form so we can bet that she is going to give all the WNBA teams all they can handle in the attempt to raise that championship trophy.

That's all for now! I'll be back in the next edition with more sports news!

The CUBB House Merch Store

Welcome to The CUBB House Merch Store! In this edition of the magazine, we are featuring these following items! Here is this edition's feature items:

For ordering, please use this link:
https://www.pandemicpresspublishing.com/the-cubb-house-merch-store/

Please include name, address, email, order details, and method of payment used.

All items can be paid by CashApp (PandemicPressMedia) or PayPal (Pandemic Press Publishing.

Any questions can be forwarded to pandemicpp@gmail.com.

Cooking Fun w/Mrs. Cubbage
Bundle Deal!
T-Shirt, Half apron, Pot holder
$40

Hello! And welcome to Fitness Facts! Where we will give you facts on fitness, to help you JUMP START your fitness program!

Well, here we are! It's the Summertime! Are you swimsuit ready? I hope so! If not, we have some easy exercises that can help you get ready for the pool, that cookout, or just hanging out.

THere are many ways that you can get a GOOD workout…you don't even have to leave your house! If you have a nice, strong, sturdy wall, you can do 'push-ups' using that wall. Make sure that you have someone with you to make sure that your back and arms are in the proper position. Then, you are ready! Try to do 3 sets of 12. It's a great alternative to getting down on the flow. (It works well if you do have trouble getting on the floor to begin with.

Good luck and keep striving for your workout goals!

(Disclaimer- Before starting any fitness program, be sure to consult with your PCP, or healthcare provider.)

Here is a great book to add to your collection:

Hey, Boy... A Tribute to My Dad, Samuel J. Cubbage Sr.

By

Samuel J. Cubbage II

This is a book done in memory of a great man, my Dad! These stories are my actual thoughts/memories that I am sharing with you, the reader. These thoughts/memories are in no particular order. But, these are the wonderful memories that I cherish of my fun-loving Dad.

Get your copy now at Lulu.com!

Looking to get your book or other item published? Well, look no further than Pandemic Press Publishing! We are Passionate about Writing, Passionate about Creativity! We are also more than just a publishing company! Contact us today for all of your needs at pandemicpp@gmail.com or visit www.pandemicpresspublishing.com!

It's official! Coming soon as part of our audio podcasts, it's The CCI Radio Show " Back To The 90s Podcast!" A great podcast with great 90s music, hosted by "Your Angel of the Airwaves," Bobbie D! It debuts soon on Blogtalkradio and where podcasts are available!

Are you looking for a little writing inspiration? Do you need some ideas for your "Great American Novel? Look no further than Pandemic Press Publishing's "Writing Inspiration!" Our tips are very informative and worth a try! Lots of tips available! Visit https://www.pandemicpresspublishing.com/ppp-writing-inspiration/ right now!

We want to take this time to say "Thank You" for reading this edition of Pandemic Press Media Magazine! (As well as the past 2022 editions!) All of your kind words and your continued support is very much appreciated and does not go unnoticed! We look forward to bringing you more great content in our next edition.

We invite you to follow and connect with our YouTube Channel, The CCI Radio Show. Please like, click, share and SUBSCRIBE! You can also listen to our secondary shows: The CCI Radio Show "Gospel Excellence w/ The Angel of the Airwaves- Bobbie D.", The CCI Radio Show "Love Notes w/ Sam C. Smooth " and The CCI Radio Show "Back To The 80s Podcast" on Blogtalkradio, Soundcloud, Spotify, Anchor Podcasts and many other social media outlets. The CCI Radio Show "TLC Podcast" is also available on our YouTube Channel! Stay Tuned!

Anything that you would like to see in our magazine? A certain recipe? Do you know someone who would like to be interviewed? Any interesting ideas at all? Let us know and we'll do our best to make it happen!

Follow Us On Social Media!

Facebook: The CCI Radio Show
Pandemic Press Publishing
Pandemic Press Media

Instagram: The CCI Radio Show
Pandemic Press Publishing
Pandemic Press Media

Twitter: The CCI Radio Show
Pandemic Press Publishing
Pandemic Press Media

YouTube: The CCI Radio Show

We are proud to announce our partnership/sponsorship

with the following company:

Follow Vybrant Souls on Instagram

Email: vybrantsouls@gmail.com

Welcome to the Pandemic Press Media family!